HORSE OR ZEBRA

BY BRENNA MALONEY

Children's Press®
An imprint of Scholastic Inc.

HORSE

A special thank-you to the team at the Cincinnati Zoo & Botanical Garden for their expert consultation.

Library of Congress Cataloging-in-Publication Data available

ISBN 978-1-338-89983-2 (library binding) | ISBN 978-1-338-89984-9 (paperback)

10 9 8 7 6 5 4 3 2 1   24 25 26 27 28

Printed in China   62
First edition, 2024

Book design by Kay Petronio

Photos ©: 5 right: Wim van den Heever/Getty Images; 6–7: Petra Tänzer/EyeEm/Getty Images; 15: Cavan Images/Getty Images; 20 main: virgonira/Getty Images; 29: Carl & Ann Purcell/Getty Images.
All other photos © Shutterstock.

ZEBRA

CONTENTS

MEET THE ANIMALS

Horses and zebras are *very* different animals. Most horses can be tamed. Zebras are wild animals. Horses can live among people. Zebras live in nature. Zebras are smaller and lighter than horses.

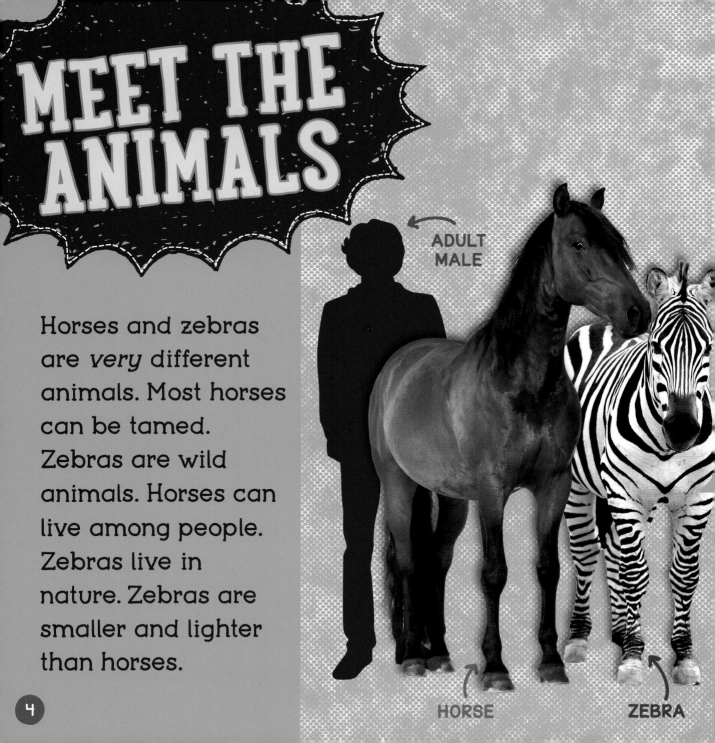

ADULT MALE

HORSE

ZEBRA

4

They have a few things in common, too. They are both **mammals**. They are also both **herd** animals. Get ready to discover more about what horses and zebras share and how they are different.

BAY HORSE

PLAINS ZEBRA

HORSE CLOSE-UP

Horses have three basic body types. Ponies are small and stocky. They are often used for riding and as pack animals. Light breeds are for riding, racing, jumping, and herding. Heavy breeds can pull plows and wagons and carry hefty loads.

WESTPHALIAN

MANE

A horse's mane is long and flowy. It can grow to several inches. The mane can give shade on hot, sunny days and keep the horse's neck warm on cold days.

TALL TAIL

A horse's tail is made from hair. It helps keep biting insects away.

COAT COLORS

Horses can be different colors and patterns. Some are black, chestnut, and gray. Some horses also have white markings on their faces and legs.

LISTEN UP!

Horse ears are short and pointed. They can move one ear at a time.

PEEPERS

A horse has the largest eyes of any land mammal. Having eyes on the sides of its head gives a horse a wide range of vision.

WHAT'S THAT SMELL?

Horses have a long nose and an excellent sense of smell.

CLIP-CLOP

To protect a horse's hooves from wear, some horses are fitted with horseshoes.

PLAINS ZEBRA

LISTEN CLOSE!

A zebra's ears are long and rounded, like a donkey's. Zebras have good hearing and can rotate their ears to locate sounds.

TOUGH TEETH

A zebra's back teeth have a wide, flat surface for chewing and crushing food.

KEEPING AN EYE OUT

A zebra's large eyes are high on its head. This helps it keep an eye out for predators, even while munching on low grasses.

HARDY HOOVES

Zebra (and horse) hooves are made of keratin, the same material in human fingernails and hair.

STRIPE SCIENCE

Scientists aren't sure why zebras are striped. The lines might confuse big predators, like lions. Since no two zebras have the same pattern, stripes may help zebras identify one another.

FLY SWATTER

Grazing animals like zebras have long, thin tails with hair on the end. Their tails are like built-in fly swatters to ward off biting insects.

SHORT AND THICK

A zebra has a thick body and shorter legs than most horses.

ZEBRA CLOSE-UP

Earth is home to three different types of zebras: the plains zebra, the Grevy's zebra, and the mountain zebra. Zebras have black and white stripes. Under their fur, their skin is black.

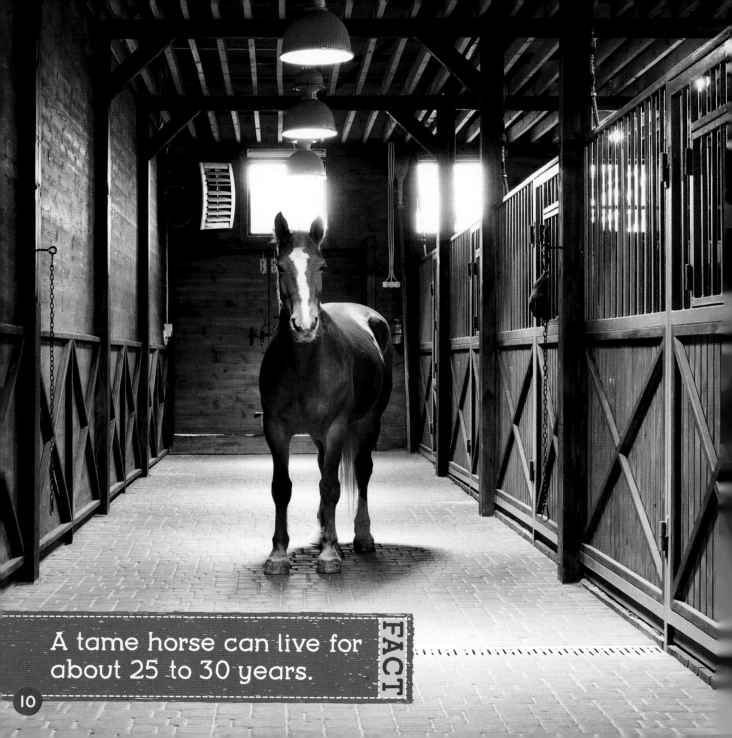

A tame horse can live for about 25 to 30 years. FACT

IN THE STABLE

Horses can be found all over the world except Antarctica and the area around the North Pole. Most horses live alongside humans and are cared for by them. Many horses live in stables, where they are protected from the wind and weather. Horses play an important role with humans. They can be used for riding, sports, farming, and police work.

IN THE WILD

Plains zebras can be found in the treeless grasslands and woodlands of eastern and southern Africa. The Grevy's zebra lives in the dry grasslands of eastern Africa. The mountain zebra is found in southern Africa. Zebras can also be found throughout the world in zoos.

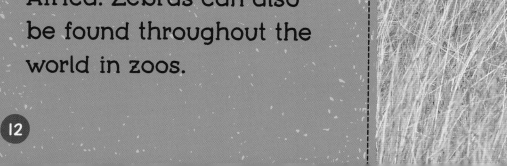

Zebras can live up to 20 years in the wild and up to almost 40 years in zoos.

HERDS AND DAZZLES

Horses are social animals. A healthy horse would never live alone by choice. When a herd of horses live together, they play with and groom one another.

Most wild horses are able to be tamed.

FACT

Zebras are also social animals. They live together in large groups called **dazzles**. Zebras are also playful! They will sometimes meet up with other grazing animals, like antelopes, and feed on grass together.

Horses are sometimes fed treats of carrots or apples.

FACT

DINING IN

Horses are **herbivores**. Their main food is grass. They also eat grains and hay, which is dried grass. An average horse needs to eat about 20 pounds (9 kg) of hay per day. The average horse will drink 5 to 10 gallons (19 to 38 liters) of fresh water per day.

DINING OUT

Zebras are also herbivores. They eat plants—mostly grasses but sometimes leaves, shrub twigs, and bark, too. Zebras spend more than half of their day eating. They are constantly on the move looking for fresh grass to eat and water to drink. Hundreds of thousands of zebras **migrate** every year in Africa. They travel in search of food and water.

Zebras need a lot of water. They can drink up to a gallon of water at one time!

Whinnies, snorts, and sniffs are just some of the noises horses and zebras use to speak. Zebras also have a high-pitched bark that sounds like a small dog.

Zebras and horses also speak with their bodies. How they hold their ears may tell you something about how they feel. If they're not happy, they put their ears back flat and show their teeth. If their ears are up and forward, they're paying attention.

FACT Zebras are known to be fierce fighters.

Horses can walk, trot, and gallop. In the trot, two hooves hit the ground at the same time, making two hoofbeats. *Clip-clop.* During a gallop, all four hooves spring off the ground at the same time.

Like horses, zebras walk, trot, and gallop. They are generally slower than horses but can run for longer periods of time. When chased, a zebra will zigzag from side to side, making it more difficult to be caught. If cornered, the zebra will rear up and kick its attacker.

When a **foal** turns one year old, it is called a yearling.

FACT

HORSE FOALS

A female horse will have a baby, or a foal, in the spring. Most horses give birth to one foal at a time. Male foals are called **colts**. Female foals are called **fillies**. Healthy foals grow quickly and can put on up to 3 pounds (more than 1 kg) a day.

ZEBRA FOALS

A zebra mother will give birth to one foal. A zebra foal is brown and white instead of black and white when it is born. Its stripes will darken over time. Most zebra babies can stand and walk within 10 to 20 minutes of birth. Within an hour or two, they can even run.

A zebra foal can weigh around 70 pounds (32 kg) at birth.

NIGHTY NIGHT

Zebras and horses can both snooze standing up. Like other hoofed animals, they have locking joints. This means they can lock their knees into position and sleep without falling over. They sleep in many short periods of rest.

YOU DECIDE!

Now you know what makes horses and zebras so different! If you had to choose, would you rather be a horse or a zebra? If you like being around people, you may choose to be a horse. If you want to be part of a dazzle, you might want to be a zebra.

Zebras don't spend a lot of time lying down. It's too dangerous around predators. In herds, the animals take turns sleeping. If one or two are lying down, other zebras remain alert.

FACT Zebras sleep for around 7 hours in a day. Horses spend 4 to 15 hours in a standing rest.

INDEX

ABOUT THE AUTHOR

Brenna Maloney is the author of many books. She lives and works in Washington, DC, with her husband, two sons, one dog, two cats, but no horses. If she had to choose, she would want to be a zebra.

GLOSSARY

colt (kohlt) – a young horse, donkey, or zebra, especially the male of such an animal

dazzle (DAZ-uhl) – a group of zebras

filly (FIL-ee) – a young female horse

foal (fohl) – a young horse, mule, donkey, or zebra

herbivore (HUR-buh-vor) – an animal that eats only plants

herd (hurd) –a large number of animals that stay together or move together

keratin (KEHR-uh-tin) – a fiber-like protein that forms the structure of feathers, hair, and nails

mammal (MAM-uhl) –a warm-blooded animal that has hair or fur and usually gives birth to live babies

migrate (MYE-grate) – to move from one area to another at a specific time of year

predator (PRED-uh-tur) –an animal that lives by hunting other animals for food